TABLE OF CONTENTS

CHAPTER 1

Understanding TikTok's Advertising Landscape

CHAPTER 2

Getting Started with TikTok Ads

CHAPTER 3

Crafting Compelling TikTok Ad Content

CHAPTER 4

TikTok Ad Campaign Strategy and Optimization

CHAPTER 5

Measuring Success and ROI

CHAPTER 6

Advanced TikTok Advertising Techniques

CHAPTER: 1

UNDERSTANDING TIKTOK'S ADVERTISING LANDSCAPE

THE RISE OF TIKTOK AS A MARKETING POWERHOUSE

In the ever-evolving landscape of digital marketing, TikTok has emerged as a formidable force, reshaping the way businesses connect with their audience. What began as a platform for short-form, user-generated content has rapidly transformed into a marketing powerhouse, offering unprecedented opportunities for brands to engage with a vast and highly active user base. With over 1 billion monthly active users and an algorithm that favors content discovery, TikTok has become a fertile ground for businesses looking to expand their reach and drive meaningful engagement.

The platform's meteoric rise as a marketing tool can be attributed to its unique blend of features that cater to both creators and advertisers. TikTok's emphasis on authentic, creative content has fostered a environment where brands can showcase their personality and connect with users on a more personal level. This shift towards more genuine, relatable marketing has resonated strongly with TikTok's predominantly younger audience, who are increasingly skeptical of traditional advertising methods. As a result, businesses that have successfully tapped into TikTok's potential have seen remarkable returns on their investment, with some campaigns going viral and generating millions of views and interactions.

As TikTok continues to evolve its advertising offerings, it has introduced a suite of tools and features designed to help businesses of all sizes leverage the platform's reach. From in-feed ads and branded hashtag challenges to influencer partnerships and shoppable content, TikTok provides a diverse array of options for marketers to craft compelling campaigns. The platform's robust analytics and targeting capabilities further enhance its appeal, allowing advertisers to fine-tune their strategies and reach their ideal audience with precision. With its rapid growth and innovative approach to social media marketing, TikTok has firmly established itself as a key player in the digital advertising space, prompting businesses across industries to reevaluate their marketing strategies and embrace this dynamic new channel.

TIKTOK'S UNIQUE AUDIENCE DEMOGRAPHICS AND BEHAVIOR

TikTok's user base is a unique and dynamic demographic that sets it apart from other social media platforms. While initially popular among Gen Z, the platform has rapidly expanded its reach to include a diverse array of age groups, with a growing presence of millennials and even older adults. This shift in demographics has created a rich tapestry of users, offering businesses unprecedented opportunities to connect with audiences across various age brackets and interests.

Understanding the behavior of TikTok users is crucial for crafting effective advertising strategies. Unlike traditional social media, TikTok's audience is characterized by its high engagement rates and preference for authentic, creative content. Users spend an average of 52 minutes per day on the app, constantly scrolling through a personalized feed of short-form videos. This behavior has fostered a culture of rapid content consumption and creation, where trends can emerge and spread globally within hours.

For businesses looking to leverage TikTok's advertising potential, it's essential to recognize the platform's unique content ecosystem. Users are not passive consumers but active participants, often engaging with branded content through challenges, duets, and user-generated content. This participatory culture presents both opportunities and challenges for advertisers, requiring a nuanced approach that balances promotional messaging with genuine entertainment value. By aligning advertising strategies with TikTok's user behavior and content preferences, businesses can tap into a highly engaged audience and achieve remarkable brand visibility and engagement.

KEY DIFFERENCES BETWEEN TIKTOK AND OTHER SOCIAL MEDIA PLATFORMS

TikTok stands out from other social media platforms in several key aspects, making it a unique and powerful tool for advertisers. Unlike Facebook or Instagram, which primarily cater to millennials and older demographics, TikTok's user base skews significantly younger, with a large portion of its audience consisting of Gen Z users. This demographic difference necessitates a shift in advertising strategies, as content that resonates with TikTok's audience often differs greatly from what works on other platforms. Additionally, TikTok's algorithm-driven content discovery system, centered around its 'For You' page, offers unparalleled potential for organic reach and virality, even for accounts with smaller followings.

Another crucial distinction lies in TikTok's content format and user behavior. While platforms like Twitter or LinkedIn focus on text-based posts and professional networking, TikTok thrives on short-form, vertical video content that's often entertaining, educational, or trend-driven. This format encourages a more immersive and engaging user experience, with the average TikTok user spending significantly more time on the app compared to other social media platforms. For advertisers, this translates to a need for creating authentic, native-feeling content that seamlessly blends with the platform's organic posts, rather than traditional, polished ad formats.

Lastly, TikTok's unique features and tools set it apart in the social media landscape. The platform's robust set of in-app editing tools, including filters, effects, and music libraries, allows for easy content creation without the need for external software. This democratization of content creation has led to a culture of authenticity and creativity that's less prevalent on other platforms. For businesses, this means that successful TikTok advertising often requires a more hands-on, creative approach, with a willingness to experiment and adapt quickly to emerging trends. Understanding these key differences is crucial for marketers looking to leverage TikTok's full potential and avoid simply repurposing strategies from other social media platforms.

THE TIKTOK ALGORITHM: HOW IT WORKS AND WHY IT MATTERS FOR ADVERTISERS

The TikTok algorithm is the beating heart of the platform's content distribution system, and understanding its intricacies is crucial for advertisers looking to make a splash in this dynamic ecosystem. At its core, the algorithm is designed to deliver highly personalized content to users, creating an addictive and engaging experience that keeps them scrolling for hours. This personalization is achieved through a complex interplay of factors, including user interactions, video information, and device settings, all of which contribute to the algorithm's decision-making process when determining which content to show to whom.

For advertisers, grasping the nuances of the TikTok algorithm is not just about gaining a competitive edge; it's about survival in an increasingly crowded digital landscape. The algorithm's preference for authentic, engaging content that resonates with users' interests means that traditional advertising approaches often fall flat on TikTok. Instead, successful advertisers must learn to create content that seamlessly blends into users' For You Page (FYP), mimicking the style and tone of organic TikTok content while still delivering their brand message. This requires a deep understanding of trending formats, popular sounds, and the types of content that typically perform well on the platform.

Moreover, the TikTok algorithm's rapid evolution and emphasis on novelty present both challenges and opportunities for advertisers. On one hand, the constant changes mean that strategies that worked yesterday may be obsolete tomorrow, requiring advertisers to stay agile and continuously adapt their approach. On the other hand, this dynamism creates a level playing field where even smaller brands can achieve viral success if they can crack the code of creating content that the algorithm favors. By leveraging data insights, staying attuned to platform trends, and consistently producing high-quality, engaging content, advertisers can position themselves to harness the full power of TikTok's algorithm and reach their target audience with unprecedented precision and impact.

CHAPTER: 2

GETTING STARTED WITH TIKTOK ADS

SETTING UP YOUR TIKTOK ADS ACCOUNT

Setting up your TikTok Ads account is the crucial first step in harnessing the platform's immense potential for business growth. As a rapidly evolving social media giant, TikTok offers a unique advertising ecosystem that requires careful navigation from the outset. This section will guide you through the process of creating and configuring your TikTok Ads account, ensuring you're well-positioned to launch effective campaigns that resonate with the platform's dynamic user base.

To begin, you'll need to visit the TikTok For Business website and click on the 'Create an Ad' button. This will prompt you to either log in with an existing TikTok account or create a new one specifically for advertising purposes. Once logged in, you'll be directed to the TikTok Ads Manager, where you'll need to provide essential information about your business, including your company name, website, and industry. It's crucial to be accurate and thorough during this setup process, as this information will influence your ad targeting options and overall campaign effectiveness.

After completing the initial setup, take the time to explore the TikTok Ads Manager interface. Familiarize yourself with key features such as the dashboard, campaign creation tools, and analytics sections. It's also advisable to link your payment method at this stage, ensuring a smooth transition when you're ready to launch your first campaign. Remember, while the setup process may seem straightforward, the decisions you make here will lay the foundation for your TikTok advertising success, so approach each step with strategic consideration.

NAVIGATING THE TIKTOK ADS MANAGER INTERFACE

Navigating the TikTok Ads Manager interface is a crucial skill for any marketer looking to harness the platform's advertising potential. At first glance, the interface may seem overwhelming, with its array of options and metrics. However, with a systematic approach, you'll find that TikTok has designed a user-friendly environment that allows for intuitive campaign creation and management. In this section, we'll break down the key components of the TikTok Ads Manager, ensuring you can confidently navigate its features to create impactful ad campaigns.

The TikTok Ads Manager is divided into several main sections, each serving a specific purpose in your advertising journey. The Dashboard provides a high-level overview of your account's performance, showcasing key metrics and recent activity. From here, you can easily access the Campaign, Ad Group, and Ad creation interfaces, where you'll spend most of your time crafting your advertising strategy. The Reporting section offers in-depth analytics, allowing you to measure the success of your campaigns and make data-driven decisions. Additionally, the Assets library helps you organize and manage your creative content, streamlining the ad creation process.

As you delve deeper into the TikTok Ads Manager, you'll discover powerful tools designed to optimize your campaigns. The

Audience Insights feature provides valuable data on your target demographics, helping you refine your targeting strategy. The Creative Tools section offers a suite of resources to enhance your ad content, including video templates and editing capabilities tailored for TikTok's unique format. By familiarizing yourself with these features and practicing within the interface, you'll soon find that creating and managing TikTok ad campaigns becomes second nature, allowing you to focus on crafting compelling content that resonates with your audience.

UNDERSTANDING TIKTOK AD FORMATS AND PLACEMENTS

TikTok's diverse array of ad formats and placements offers businesses unparalleled opportunities to engage with their target audience on this dynamic platform. From In-Feed Ads that seamlessly blend into users' For You Page to TopView Ads that capture attention the moment the app is opened, each format serves a unique purpose in your marketing strategy. Understanding these options is crucial for crafting campaigns that resonate with TikTok's predominantly young, tech-savvy user base while aligning with your brand's objectives and message.

Brand Takeover Ads and Branded Effects provide immersive experiences that can significantly boost brand awareness and user engagement. These high-impact formats allow for creative storytelling and user interaction, fostering a deeper connection between your brand and TikTok's community. Meanwhile, Hashtag Challenges offer a powerful way to generate user-generated content and viral trends, leveraging the platform's inherent shareability to amplify your reach exponentially.

Choosing the right combination of ad formats and placements requires a strategic approach, taking into account factors such as campaign goals, target demographics, and budget constraints. By mastering TikTok's diverse advertising ecosystem, businesses can create multi-faceted campaigns that drive real results, whether it's increasing brand visibility, driving website traffic, or boosting conversions. As we delve deeper into each format, you'll gain the insights needed to craft TikTok ad strategies that not only capture attention but also deliver measurable business outcomes in this fast-paced digital landscape.

DEFINING YOUR ADVERTISING GOALS AND KPIS

Defining clear advertising goals and key performance indicators (KPIs) is the cornerstone of any successful TikTok ad campaign. As a business venturing into the dynamic world of TikTok, it's crucial to align your advertising objectives with your overall marketing strategy. Whether you're aiming to boost brand awareness, drive website traffic, or increase conversions, setting specific, measurable, achievable, relevant, and time-bound (SMART) goals will provide a roadmap for your TikTok advertising journey.

Once you've established your goals, identifying the right KPIs becomes essential for tracking and measuring your campaign's success. For brand awareness campaigns, metrics such as video views, engagement rates, and follower growth can provide valuable insights. If your focus is on driving conversions, you'll want to pay close attention to click-through rates, cost per acquisition, and return on ad spend. By carefully selecting and monitoring these KPIs, you'll be able to optimize your TikTok ad performance and make data-driven decisions to maximize your return on investment.

It's important to remember that TikTok's unique audience and platform characteristics may require you to adapt your traditional advertising metrics. For instance, the platform's emphasis on authentic, creative content means that engagement rates and user-generated content metrics might carry more weight than on other social media platforms. As you define your goals and KPIs, consider how TikTok's fast-paced, trend-driven environment aligns with your business objectives, and be prepared to adjust your strategies as you gain more insights into what resonates with your target audience on this innovative platform.

CHAPTER: 3

CRAFTING COMPELLING TIKTOK AD CONTENT

THE ART OF CREATING SCROLL-STOPPING TIKTOK VIDEOS

In the fast-paced world of TikTok, capturing users' attention is both an art and a science. Creating scroll-stopping videos requires a deep understanding of the platform's unique ecosystem and user behavior. As a marketer or business owner, your primary goal is to craft content that not only stands out in the crowded TikTok feed but also resonates with your target audience, compelling them to engage with your ad and take action.

To achieve this, it's crucial to leverage TikTok's native features and trending formats. Incorporate popular music, filters, and effects that align with your brand message and appeal to your audience. Remember, authenticity is key on TikTok – users can spot overly polished, inauthentic content from a mile away. Instead, focus on creating relatable, entertaining, or informative videos that provide value to viewers while subtly showcasing your product or service.

Timing is everything when it comes to TikTok ads. The first few seconds of your video are critical in determining whether a user will continue watching or scroll past. Hook your audience immediately with a compelling visual, an intriguing question, or a surprising statement. Then, maintain that engagement throughout the video with a clear, concise message and a strong call-to-action. By mastering these elements, you'll be well on your way to creating TikTok ads that not only stop the scroll but also drive meaningful results for your business.

LEVERAGING TRENDS, CHALLENGES, AND HASHTAGS IN YOUR ADS

In the fast-paced world of TikTok, trends, challenges, and hashtags are the lifeblood of viral content. As a savvy advertiser, leveraging these elements in your TikTok ads can significantly boost engagement and reach. By aligning your ad content with current trends, you tap into the collective consciousness of the platform's user base, making your message more relatable and shareable. This strategy not only increases the likelihood of your ad resonating with viewers but also positions your brand as current and in-tune with the TikTok community.

Challenges, in particular, offer a unique opportunity for brands to encourage user-generated content and foster a sense of community around their products or services. By creating or participating in challenges that align with your brand values, you can inspire TikTok users to interact with your ad content in a more meaningful way. This interactive approach not only amplifies your reach but also builds authentic connections with potential customers, turning passive viewers into active participants in your brand story.

Hashtags, the unsung heroes of discoverability on TikTok, play a crucial role in expanding your ad's visibility. By strategically incorporating trending and relevant hashtags into your ad content, you increase the chances of your message reaching beyond your immediate target audience. However, it's essential to strike a balance between popular, broad hashtags and more niche, industry-specific ones to ensure your content reaches the right viewers. Remember, the key to success on TikTok lies in authenticity and creativity – use these elements to craft ads that seamlessly blend with organic content while still delivering your brand message effectively.

COLLABORATING WITH TIKTOK INFLUENCERS FOR MAXIMUM IMPACT

Collaborating with TikTok influencers has become an essential strategy for businesses looking to maximize their impact on the platform. These content creators have already built substantial followings and understand the nuances of what resonates with TikTok's unique audience. By partnering with the right influencers, brands can tap into pre-existing communities, leveraging the trust and engagement these creators have cultivated with their followers. This approach not only extends your reach but also lends authenticity to your message, as influencers can seamlessly integrate your product or service into their content in a way that feels natural and relatable to their audience.

When selecting influencers for collaboration, it's crucial to look beyond mere follower counts. The most effective partnerships arise when there's a genuine alignment between the influencer's content style, values, and audience demographics with your brand's identity and target market. Micro-influencers, for instance, often boast higher engagement rates and more niche audiences, which can lead to more meaningful interactions and conversions for your campaigns. As you embark on influencer collaborations, be prepared to give creators a degree of creative freedom; their understanding of their audience and the platform's trends can lead to content that performs exceptionally well, often surpassing traditional ad formats in terms of engagement and conversion rates.

To maximize the impact of influencer collaborations, consider integrating them into a broader TikTok advertising strategy. This could involve using influencer-created content in your paid ad campaigns, co-creating branded hashtag challenges, or leveraging influencer partnerships to drive traffic to your TikTok shop. By combining the organic reach of influencers with the targeting capabilities of TikTok's ad platform, you can create a powerful synergy that amplifies your message and drives tangible business results. Remember, the key to success lies in fostering authentic, long-term relationships with influencers who genuinely resonate with your brand, rather than pursuing one-off transactions that may lack depth and credibility in the eyes of the TikTok community.

BEST PRACTICES FOR TIKTOK AD COPYWRITING AND CALL-TO-ACTIONS

Crafting compelling ad copy for TikTok requires a unique approach that aligns with the platform's fast-paced, creative nature. Unlike traditional advertising channels, TikTok demands concise, punchy, and highly engaging content that can capture users' attention within seconds. The key to success lies in understanding the platform's predominantly young audience and their preference for authentic, relatable content. When writing ad copy for TikTok, focus on creating short, catchy phrases that resonate with your target demographic and reflect the latest trends and viral challenges on the platform.

Effective call-to-actions (CTAs) on TikTok should be clear, direct, and inspire immediate action. Given the platform's short-form video format, it's crucial to integrate your CTA seamlessly into the content, making it feel like a natural part of the user's viewing experience. Experiment with creative CTAs that go beyond the standard 'Buy Now' or 'Learn More' - instead, try phrases like 'Join the Challenge,' 'Duet with Us,' or 'Show Us Your Skills.' These action-oriented CTAs not only encourage engagement but also leverage TikTok's unique features, fostering a sense of community and participation among users.

To maximize the impact of your TikTok ad copy and CTAs,

it's essential to continuously test and refine your approach. Utilize TikTok's robust analytics tools to track the performance of different copy variations and CTA styles. Pay close attention to metrics such as view-through rate, engagement rate, and conversion rate to identify what resonates best with your audience. Remember, the TikTok landscape evolves rapidly, so stay agile and be prepared to adapt your copywriting strategies as new trends emerge. By combining data-driven insights with creative, platform-specific content, you'll be well-positioned to create TikTok ads that not only capture attention but also drive meaningful business results.

CHAPTER: 4

TIKTOK AD CAMPAIGN STRATEGY AND OPTIMIZATION

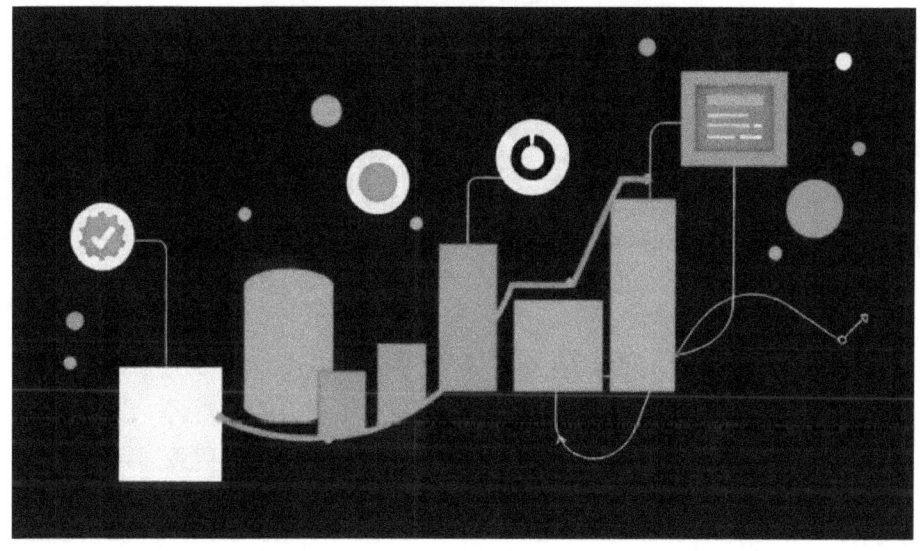

TARGETING AND AUDIENCE SEGMENTATION ON TIKTOK

Targeting and audience segmentation on TikTok are crucial elements for any successful ad campaign on this rapidly evolving platform. Unlike traditional social media, TikTok's algorithm-driven content discovery mechanism presents unique opportunities and challenges for advertisers. Understanding how to leverage TikTok's robust targeting options can significantly enhance your campaign's effectiveness, ensuring your message reaches the right users at the right time.

TikTok offers a variety of targeting parameters, including demographics, interests, behaviors, and custom audiences. However, the platform's strength lies in its ability to reach users based on their engagement with specific types of content, rather than just static profile information. This dynamic targeting approach allows advertisers to tap into the platform's viral nature, reaching users who are most likely to engage with and share their content. By carefully segmenting your audience and tailoring your creative approach to each segment, you can maximize the impact of your TikTok ad spend and drive meaningful results for your business.

One of the most powerful targeting features on TikTok is the 'Custom Audience' option, which allows advertisers to reach users who have already interacted with their brand, either on TikTok or through other channels. This can include website visitors, app users, or customer lists from your CRM. By combining these custom audiences with TikTok's 'Lookalike Audiences' feature, you can expand your reach to new users who share similar characteristics with your best customers, effectively scaling your campaigns while maintaining relevance. As we delve deeper into TikTok's targeting capabilities, we'll explore strategies for creating and optimizing these audience segments to drive maximum ROI for your advertising efforts.

BUDGETING AND BIDDING STRATEGIES FOR TIKTOK ADS

Mastering the art of budgeting and bidding on TikTok is crucial for maximizing your advertising ROI. Unlike traditional platforms, TikTok's unique algorithm and user behavior patterns require a nuanced approach to resource allocation. This section will guide you through the intricacies of setting up a cost-effective budget that aligns with your campaign goals, while also exploring the various bidding strategies available on the platform.

When it comes to budgeting, it's essential to start with a clear understanding of your overall marketing objectives and how TikTok fits into your broader strategy. We'll explore how to determine the optimal daily or lifetime budget for your campaigns, taking into account factors such as audience size, campaign duration, and desired reach. Additionally, we'll delve into the importance of allocating funds for testing and optimization, ensuring that you have the flexibility to refine your approach as you gather data on ad performance.

TikTok offers several bidding strategies, each suited to different campaign objectives and stages of the customer journey. We'll examine the pros and cons of cost-per-mille (CPM), cost-per-click (CPC), and cost-per-acquisition (CPA) bidding models, providing you with the insights needed to choose the most appropriate strategy for your specific goals. Furthermore, we'll discuss advanced techniques such as bid capping and pacing, which can help you maintain control over your spending while maximizing the impact of your TikTok ad campaigns.

A/B TESTING AND PERFORMANCE ANALYSIS

A/B testing is a crucial component of any successful TikTok ad campaign strategy. By creating multiple versions of your ads and comparing their performance, you can identify which elements resonate most with your target audience. This data-driven approach allows you to optimize your campaigns for maximum engagement, conversions, and return on investment. When conducting A/B tests on TikTok, focus on variables such as ad creative, copy, call-to-action buttons, and targeting parameters to uncover the winning combinations that drive results.

Performance analysis goes hand-in-hand with A/B testing, providing valuable insights into the effectiveness of your TikTok ad campaigns. Utilize TikTok's robust analytics tools to track key metrics such as view-through rate, engagement rate, click-through rate, and conversion rate. By regularly monitoring these metrics, you can identify trends, spot areas for improvement, and make data-informed decisions to refine your ad strategy. Remember that TikTok's algorithm and user behavior can change rapidly, so staying agile and responsive to performance data is essential for maintaining campaign success.

To maximize the impact of your A/B testing and performance analysis efforts, establish a systematic approach to experimentation and optimization. Set clear objectives for each test, determine statistically significant sample sizes, and allow sufficient time for meaningful data collection. Don't be afraid to test bold, creative ideas alongside more conservative approaches – TikTok's unique audience often responds well to innovative content. By continuously iterating and refining your campaigns based on performance data, you'll be well-positioned to stay ahead of the competition and achieve long-term success on this dynamic platform.

SCALING SUCCESSFUL CAMPAIGNS AND MANAGING AD FATIGUE

Scaling successful TikTok ad campaigns requires a delicate balance of persistence and innovation. As your initial campaigns gain traction and deliver results, it's tempting to simply increase your budget and let them run indefinitely. However, the rapid-fire nature of TikTok's content consumption means that ad fatigue can set in quickly, potentially diminishing your return on investment. To combat this, marketers must adopt a proactive approach, constantly monitoring performance metrics and user engagement levels to identify the early signs of campaign fatigue.

When scaling your TikTok ad campaigns, it's crucial to implement a strategy of continuous optimization and creative refreshment. This involves regularly updating your ad content with new visuals, sounds, and messaging that align with current trends and user preferences on the platform. By maintaining a diverse ad portfolio and rotating creatives frequently, you can keep your audience engaged and prevent the onset of ad fatigue. Additionally, leveraging TikTok's advanced targeting options allows you to expand your reach to new, relevant audience segments, further extending the life and effectiveness of your campaigns.

Managing ad fatigue on TikTok also requires a keen

understanding of the platform's unique ecosystem and user behavior patterns. Unlike traditional advertising channels, TikTok's algorithm-driven content discovery means that users are constantly exposed to new and diverse content. As a result, advertisers must strive to create ads that feel native to the platform and blend seamlessly with organic content. This approach not only helps maintain user interest but also improves the overall performance of your campaigns. By striking the right balance between scaling your successful ads and introducing fresh, innovative content, you can maximize the longevity and impact of your TikTok advertising efforts.

CHAPTER: 5

MEASURING SUCCESS AND ROI

KEY METRICS AND ANALYTICS FOR TIKTOK AD CAMPAIGNS

In the fast-paced world of TikTok advertising, understanding and leveraging key metrics and analytics is crucial for campaign success. As a marketer or business owner, you need to navigate through a sea of data to identify what truly matters for your TikTok ad campaigns. This section will demystify the essential metrics and analytics tools that TikTok provides, empowering you to make data-driven decisions and optimize your advertising efforts for maximum impact.

TikTok offers a robust suite of analytics tools that provide valuable insights into your ad performance. From basic metrics like views, likes, and shares to more advanced indicators such as click-through rates (CTR), conversion rates, and return on ad spend (ROAS), we'll explore how each metric contributes to your overall campaign success. By understanding these key performance indicators (KPIs), you'll be able to gauge the effectiveness of your ads, identify areas for improvement, and refine your strategies to achieve better results over time.

Beyond the numbers, we'll delve into how to interpret these metrics in the context of your specific business goals and target audience. You'll learn how to set up custom conversion events, track user behavior, and utilize TikTok's Pixel technology to gain deeper insights into your audience's journey from ad view to purchase. By mastering these analytics, you'll be well-equipped to measure your TikTok advertising success accurately and demonstrate a clear ROI to stakeholders, ensuring your campaigns not only resonate with users but also drive tangible business outcomes.

INTEGRATING TIKTOK ADS WITH YOUR OVERALL MARKETING STRATEGY

Integrating TikTok ads into your overall marketing strategy is crucial for maximizing the platform's potential and achieving synergy across your digital presence. While TikTok's unique features and audience demographics may seem distinct from other social media platforms, it's essential to view it as a complementary piece of your broader marketing puzzle. By aligning your TikTok ad campaigns with your existing marketing efforts, you can create a cohesive brand message that resonates across multiple channels, reinforcing your brand identity and amplifying your reach.

To effectively integrate TikTok ads, start by identifying overlapping goals and themes between your TikTok strategy and other marketing initiatives. For instance, if you're running a cross-platform campaign focused on user-generated content, consider how TikTok's Hashtag Challenges can amplify this effort. Similarly, leverage TikTok's robust targeting capabilities to retarget users who have engaged with your brand on other platforms, creating a seamless customer journey. Remember, the key is to maintain consistency in your brand voice and messaging while adapting to TikTok's unique, creative, and fast-paced environment.

Measuring the impact of your integrated strategy is crucial for ongoing optimization. Utilize TikTok's analytics tools in conjunction with your existing marketing metrics to gain a holistic view of campaign performance. Pay close attention to how TikTok ads influence metrics on other platforms, such as website traffic, engagement rates, or conversion rates. This data-driven approach will allow you to refine your integrated strategy over time, ensuring that your TikTok ads not only perform well in isolation but also contribute meaningfully to your overall marketing objectives. By mastering this integration, you'll be well-positioned to leverage TikTok's explosive growth while maintaining a cohesive and effective marketing presence across all channels.

ATTRIBUTION MODELING AND CROSS-PLATFORM PERFORMANCE TRACKING

In the rapidly evolving landscape of digital advertising, understanding the true impact of your TikTok ad campaigns is crucial for optimizing performance and maximizing ROI. Attribution modeling plays a pivotal role in this process, allowing marketers to accurately measure the contribution of various touchpoints along the customer journey. By implementing sophisticated attribution models, businesses can gain valuable insights into how TikTok ads interact with other marketing channels, ultimately leading to more informed decision-making and improved campaign effectiveness.

Cross-platform performance tracking takes this analysis a step further, enabling advertisers to holistically evaluate their marketing efforts across multiple platforms. This comprehensive approach is particularly important when integrating TikTok ads into a broader digital strategy. By leveraging advanced analytics tools and data integration techniques, marketers can create a unified view of their customers' interactions across TikTok, other social media platforms, websites, and offline touchpoints. This holistic perspective not only helps in accurately attributing conversions but also in identifying synergies between different marketing channels, leading to more efficient budget allocation and improved overall campaign performance.

To effectively implement attribution modeling and cross-platform tracking for TikTok ads, marketers should focus on selecting the right attribution model that aligns with their business goals and customer journey. Whether opting for a last-click, first-click, or multi-touch attribution model, the key is to consistently apply this methodology across all platforms for accurate comparisons. Additionally, investing in robust analytics tools that can seamlessly integrate data from TikTok Ads Manager with other marketing platforms is essential. By mastering these advanced measurement techniques, businesses can unlock the full potential of their TikTok advertising efforts, driving growth and staying ahead in the competitive digital landscape.

CALCULATING AND IMPROVING RETURN ON AD SPEND (ROAS)

Calculating Return on Ad Spend (ROAS) is a crucial metric for measuring the success of your TikTok advertising campaigns. ROAS is determined by dividing the revenue generated from your ads by the amount spent on those ads, providing a clear picture of your campaign's profitability. For instance, if you spent $1,000 on TikTok ads and generated $5,000 in sales, your ROAS would be 5:1, indicating a strong return on your investment. Regularly monitoring your ROAS allows you to make data-driven decisions about your ad strategy and budget allocation.

Improving your ROAS on TikTok requires a multifaceted approach that combines creative content, precise targeting, and continuous optimization. Start by crafting engaging, native-feeling content that resonates with TikTok's unique audience, ensuring your ads don't feel out of place in users' feeds. Leverage TikTok's robust targeting options to reach the most relevant audience for your product or service, and experiment with different ad formats to find what works best for your brand. Additionally, use A/B testing to refine your ad elements, such as captions, calls-to-action, and visual components, to maximize engagement and conversions.

To truly master ROAS optimization on TikTok, it's essential to look beyond the platform itself and consider the entire customer journey. Ensure your landing pages are optimized for mobile and provide a seamless user experience, as a significant portion of

TikTok traffic comes from mobile devices. Implement retargeting strategies to re-engage users who have shown interest but haven't converted, and consider using influencer partnerships to boost credibility and reach. By continuously analyzing your campaign data, staying agile in your approach, and aligning your TikTok strategy with your overall marketing goals, you can steadily improve your ROAS and achieve sustainable growth on this dynamic platform.

CHAPTER: 6

ADVANCED TIKTOK ADVERTISING TECHNIQUES

LEVERAGING TIKTOK'S E-COMMERCE FEATURES FOR DIRECT SALES

TikTok's e-commerce features have revolutionized the way businesses approach direct sales on social media platforms. With its seamless integration of shopping capabilities, TikTok has created a powerful ecosystem where brands can showcase products, engage with potential customers, and drive conversions all within the app. This chapter will explore how businesses can leverage TikTok's e-commerce tools to maximize their sales potential and create a frictionless shopping experience for their audience.

One of the key advantages of TikTok's e-commerce features is the ability to create shoppable videos that allow users to purchase products without leaving the platform. By utilizing TikTok's product tagging system, businesses can highlight specific items within their content, providing viewers with instant access to product information and purchase options. This seamless integration of content and commerce not only enhances the user experience but also significantly reduces the steps between discovery and purchase, leading to higher conversion rates and increased sales.

To fully capitalize on TikTok's e-commerce potential, businesses must adopt a strategic approach that combines compelling content creation with smart use of the platform's sales tools. This includes leveraging features such as live shopping events, where brands can showcase products in real-time and interact directly with potential customers, answering questions and addressing concerns on the spot. By mastering these techniques, businesses can create a dynamic and engaging shopping experience that resonates with TikTok's user base and drives tangible results in the form of increased sales and customer loyalty.

RETARGETING STRATEGIES ON TIKTOK

Retargeting on TikTok represents a powerful strategy for businesses looking to maximize their advertising ROI. By leveraging the platform's sophisticated pixel technology and machine learning algorithms, advertisers can re-engage users who have previously interacted with their brand, website, or app. This approach allows for highly personalized ad experiences, increasing the likelihood of conversion and fostering stronger customer relationships.

To implement effective retargeting campaigns on TikTok, businesses must first ensure proper pixel implementation and audience segmentation. By categorizing users based on their previous interactions - such as video views, profile visits, or specific actions taken on your website - you can tailor your ad content to address their unique interests and position in the customer journey. This level of customization not only improves ad relevance but also significantly boosts engagement rates and overall campaign performance.

One of TikTok's standout features for retargeting is its ability to create lookalike audiences based on your existing customer data. By analyzing the characteristics and behaviors of your most valuable customers, TikTok's AI can identify similar users within its vast user base, effectively expanding your reach to high-potential prospects. This powerful combination of retargeting and lookalike audience creation allows businesses to build comprehensive, multi-touchpoint campaigns that guide users through the entire marketing funnel, from awareness to conversion.

CREATING AND OPTIMIZING TIKTOK LANDING PAGES

Creating an effective landing page for your TikTok ads is crucial for converting viewers into customers. Unlike traditional websites, TikTok landing pages need to be fast-loading, mobile-optimized, and designed to capture the attention of a younger, more dynamic audience. The key is to maintain the same energy and style as your TikTok content, ensuring a seamless transition from ad to landing page that doesn't disrupt the user's experience.

Optimization is an ongoing process that requires constant testing and refinement. A/B testing different elements such as headlines, call-to-action buttons, and visual layouts can provide valuable insights into what resonates best with your TikTok audience. Pay close attention to load times, as even a one-second delay can significantly impact conversion rates. Incorporate social proof, such as user-generated content or testimonials, to build trust and credibility with your TikTok-savvy visitors.

To maximize conversions, your TikTok landing page should be laser-focused on a single objective, whether it's collecting email addresses, driving app downloads, or making sales. Remove any unnecessary distractions and ensure that your value proposition is clearly communicated within seconds of landing on the page. Remember, TikTok users are accustomed to quick, engaging content, so your landing page should reflect this preference for brevity and impact. By aligning your landing page strategy with the unique characteristics of the TikTok platform, you'll be well-positioned to turn your ad views into tangible business results.

FUTURE TRENDS AND EMERGING OPPORTUNITIES IN TIKTOK ADVERTISING

As we look to the horizon of TikTok advertising, several emerging trends and opportunities are poised to reshape the landscape for businesses. Artificial Intelligence and Machine Learning are set to play an increasingly pivotal role, with TikTok's algorithms becoming even more sophisticated in targeting and content delivery. This advancement will likely lead to hyper-personalized ad experiences, where each user receives content tailored not just to their demographics, but to their real-time mood and context.

Another frontier in TikTok advertising lies in the realm of Augmented Reality (AR) and Virtual Reality (VR). As these technologies mature, we can expect to see a surge in immersive ad formats that blur the lines between entertainment and marketing. Imagine virtual try-ons for fashion brands or AR-powered product demonstrations that users can interact with in their own spaces. These innovations will not only boost engagement but also provide valuable data on user preferences and behaviors.

Lastly, the integration of e-commerce functionalities directly within TikTok ads is set to revolutionize social commerce. We're moving towards a future where the path from discovery to purchase is seamless and instantaneous. Live shopping events, shoppable videos, and in-app checkout features will become standard, turning TikTok into a powerful sales channel. Businesses that can master these emerging opportunities will find themselves at the forefront of a new era in digital advertising, where creativity, technology, and commerce converge to create unparalleled growth potential.

www.ingramcontent.com/pod-product-compliance
Lightning Source LLC
Chambersburg PA
CBHW070939220526
45469CB00007B/2445